Soccer Coach!
A Survival Manual

By

ISBN 0-9716382-4-1

WARNING-DISCLAIMER

TABLE OF CONTENTS

INTRODUCTION

This is a simple, no-nonsense soccer-coaching manual for those of you who have found yourselves suddenly faced with the task of coaching a soccer team. Whether you have a recreational, competitive youth team, or an adult league team, these fundamental skills and drills apply to all levels. The purpose of this book is to introduce you to key fundamental skills that successful soccer players, from recreational to professional, have as a foundation for this sport as well as offer guidelines for managing your team. These techniques are presented in easy to understand language that is clear and to the point. Additionally, the techniques, drills, checklists, warm-ups, and game plans highlighted in this manual were chosen based on over twenty years of testing in the only true soccer laboratory... *the soccer field!*

This manual also assumes that many of you have not had the opportunity or time, and still do not, to learn these techniques. By following the step-by-step descriptions and illustrations, you should be able to teach these techniques and drills to your players. **Hint**: always keep an eye out for a player on your team who may already be able to perform these techniques and use him/her to demonstrate for you.

In the chapter titled "Three Month Training Schedule", the practice drills and routines are structured so each training session reinforces the previous one. This is why you will notice repetition with the introduction of a new element each session. There is also room to insert your own drills in order to encourage and reinforce your own unique coaching style.

Descriptions are as brief as possible for quick understanding and later reference. Photographs are added for additional clarification.

There are many books available with hundreds of drills, game analysis, and skill development techniques. These publications are helpful and valuable in what they offer to the soccer coach and player. The *Survival Manual* covers most areas of concern for new and experienced coaches and provides you with a <u>complete</u> program – especially for new coaches. Additionally, the *Survival Manual* is set-up to give you a quick and efficient method for putting together a successful soccer team as soon as possible while, at the same time, building and reinforcing good soccer habits in players.

A new addition to this manual is the Goalkeeper Chapter. There are 21 new photographs demonstrating various goalkeeping techniques and positions to aid you in effectively coaching your young players. Additionally, I recommend Tony Waiters' books, as he has proven himself at the international level and is committed to proper development of youth soccer players.

I hope you find *Soccer Coach! A Survival Manual* effective in helping you quickly establish a quality team with a strong foundation in individual and team skills. I encourage constructive feedback in order to improve revisions. Contact information is at the back of this manual in the Background

Chapter 1

<u>Skills</u>

<u>Inside of Foot Technique</u>

The Bread and Butter of the soccer player

Why teach this technique . . .?

Look closely at any professional, college, or high level high school and club soccer game and the skill used more often than any other is the *inside of the foot* technique. It is the safest and most accurate way to trap the ball, pass the ball, and even shoot the ball. Once a soccer player masters this basic skill, mistakes in passing, trapping, and shooting will be minimized resulting in his or her confidence level on the field, under pressure, skyrocketing!

Skill

*The Steps for Mastering the **Inside of Foot** Technique*

1. Foot is off the ground about six inches.
2. Toes are up higher than the heel.
3. Foot is angled out 90 degrees.
4. The ankle is *locked* or *stiff.*
5. Feet are shoulder width apart.
6. While executing skill, knees are bent.

(See photos on following page)

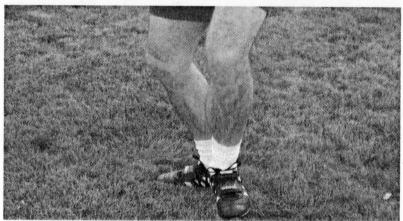

Helpful Hints

*Both knees are bent for agility and relaxation.
*Flair arms out for balance.
*Picture the passing foot looking/acting as a golf putter.
*Keep the kicking foot *90 degrees* to the planted foot.
*Kicking foot should be positioned about shoulder
  width away from the planting foot.

Inside of Foot *Passing*

Skill

1. With foot in *putter position* described above, kick a stationary ball.
2. *Punch* the ball with foot.
3. Keep toes *above* the heel during kick.
4. Drop foot only after ball has traveled a yard or two.

<u>Helpful Hints</u>

*Keep knees bent, arms flared out for balance and good form.
*Foot is up off the ground *directly behind* middle of ball before
  making contact.
*Foot also stays off the ground just after contact to ensure
  proper movement through the *middle* of the ball..
***Extremely Important**: to ensure accuracy, keep kicking foot in 90
  degree position and toe up above heel while kicking the ball!
*Insist on good quality technique practice -

Practice Makes Permanent!

<u>Inside of Foot *Trapping*</u>

Note: This technique is the same as the previous skill except the player is *stopping* the ball instead of passing it. Body and foot position, as described above, is the same.

Skill

1. Player moves into the direct path of the ball.
2. Trapping foot is approximately six inches off the ground **before** the ball arrives and makes contact.
3. Player must watch the ball all the way to making contact with the trapping foot.
4. The trapping foot absorbs the speed of the ball by **moving back wards** just as the ball hits the foot. The foot acts like a shock absorber.

<u>Helpful Hints</u>

*Move early to get behind the path of the ball.
**Do not take eyes off the ball!* (otherwise, you may
mis-trap it.)
*Maintain Good Form:
      1. Toes up, heel down.
      2. Trapping foot 90 degrees to planted foot.
      3. Knees bent, arms out for balance.

Inside of Foot *Shooting*

Skill

1. This technique is the same as the *Inside of Foot Passing*, except the player is simply "shooting" the ball into the net.
2. As with passing and trapping, this technique is the safest and surest way to score a goal for short range shots (scoring this way may not look dramatic, but it gets results).
3. A ball shot on the ground, several feet to either side of a goal keeper, is one of the most difficult shots to stop - *ask any expe rienced goalkeeper!*

Power Shooting using the *Instep*

Note: Along with the "safe" *Inside of Foot Shot*, the most powerful and natural shot is the **Instep Shot**. The *instep* is located on the top of the foot where your shoelaces are located. Essentially, it is the same movement used in the game of *kickball* and for Field Goals and PATs in football. The most important characteristic of the *Instep Shot* is to keep the ball **low to the ground** when shooting.

Skill

1. As the player approaches the ball, the planting foot is even with the ball and about 10 inches out to the side.
2. Cock the kicking leg back to where heel almost strikes the butt cheek.
3. The position of the head should be *over/above* the ball.
4. It is important to snap the kicking leg down.
5. The toes of the kicking foot are pointed down, locking the ankle. Instruct your players to push their toes down into the sole of their shoe as hard as they can. This will automatically lock their ankle.
6. The head stays over the ball with *eyes on the ball **until** the foot makes contact with the ball!*
7. The toes stay pointed with ankle locked on follow-through.
   (see photo on following page)

<u>Helpful Hints</u>

*If planting foot is too close to the ball, this will cause a miskick.

*For a right-footed kick: lean left, away from the ball when planting.

*For a left-footed kick: lean right, away from the ball when planting.

*Be sure kicking foot comes all the way back and hits the butt cheek.

Do not lean back when kicking or ball will lift too high in the air.

*The snap of the kicking leg comes from the knee down.

*Toes ***must be pointed*** to get low drive and maximum power.

*Eyes ***must watch foot hit the ball*** or ball will be miskicked.

*Toes down and locked after kick ensures a low, powerful shot!

<u>Dribbling</u>

Skill

Controlling the Ball:

1. In most areas on the field, the ball should be dribbled close to the body.
2. To dribble close is to touch or push the ball about every one or two steps. The steps are short, choppy steps staying on the toes as much as possible.
3. By keeping the weight of the body on the balls of the feet (staying on the toes), a player is ready to react to unpredictable bounces and direction changes of the ball as well as quickly react to an opponent in order to shield or protect the ball.
4. Whether using the *Inside of Foot* or the *Instep* to dribble the ball, the ball should be "pushed" or "stroked" with the foot. The touch of the ball must be gentle, not hard, in order to keep the ball close.
5. In open areas such as the flanks or outside areas of the field, the player can push the ball further in front (about four to five feet) in order to move faster.
6. Eyes should be focused about three feet in front of the ball with quick glances up and around to locate the position of teammates and opponents.

Helpful Hints

- Ball is kept close to feet to protect it from opponents.
- Keeping the ball close allows for quick changes of direction.
- Discourage players from kicking the ball and chasing after it. If a ball is more than a player's leg reach away, an opponent who is close by can intercept and steal the ball away. *The further away from the foot, the higher chance of losing the ball to an opponent.*
- The flanks and open field (breakaways to the 'keeper, gaps in the other team between **defense - midfield** or **midfield - offense**) are the safest places for pushing the ball four to five feet in front of player in order to move faster.
- By focusing in front of the ball while dribbling, instead of only on the ball, a player becomes aware of a larger area around him/her and will develop better vision on the field. Inexperienced players have a tendency to look only at the ball when dribbling, unable to see other players and how the flow of the game is changing. By looking up and in front of the ball, a player can still see the ball at the bottom of his/her peripheral vision yet also see a wider area above and to the sides of the peripheral area.

Chapter 2

Small-sided Games

Various Types and Their Effectiveness

Note: Small-sided games are becoming more and more popular at youth and adult practices. They allow for more touches of the ball by each player than full eleven-a-side games. Small-sided games also develop, in a natural way, important aspects of body position in relation to teammates and to the ball.

Perhaps, the biggest bonus of the small-sided game is its reproduction of the old-fashioned *pick-up* game played in the streets and vacant lots of America. *Pick-up* games are the way most kids around the world learn the natural ebb and flow of the game of soccer and develop familiarity with ball handling. This is no different than those baseball, softball, football, and basketball games we have seen or been a part of on streets, cul de sacs, vacant lots, and fields for decades. It is the incubator for the *natural* development of any game involving development of motor skills.

Accordingly, most professional soccer teams around the world integrate small-sided games of various sorts into their daily practice schedules. Each small-sided game is a great fitness workout for *all* players. Why? Because the ball is touched more often by **each** player, forcing him or her to work harder, instead of standing and watching the game. Also, small-sided games, as mentioned above, allow every player (goalkeepers too!) more touches of the ball in a realistic game environment (pressure situations), giving ample opportunity to get comfortable moving a ball with the foot.

Small-sided games are also great for giving young soccer players a way to develop individual skills and *fancy footwork* in a natural setting. Normally, this type of creative development, usually found primarily in pick-up games, is recreated in the small-sided games. The beauty of the small-sided practice game lies in its ability to cover various aspects of the game of soccer all at once, which is the way an actual game develops, changes, and flows during regulation time.

Types of *Small-Sided Games*

3 v 3

- Three players on each team. No goalkeepers.
- In place of goalkeepers, one cone or bag as target on each end of small field.
- Mark out with different cones a field of 35 x 20 yards.
- To score a goal, each team must hit a cone.
- Limit game time to four minutes, then a five-minute water break, then play again.

Challenges for Development or Progression to Increase Difficulty:

a. each team must make 3 passes before shooting at cone/bag to score.

b. come up with your own variations using above guidelines as a foundation.

c. all passes must be Inside of Foot to be counted as good pass es.

Helpful Hints

• If cone/bag is too hard to hit, make small goal about 3 feet wide to pass ball through.

• 3 v 3 is the most demanding, physically, of small-sided games because fewer players equals more work per player.

4 v 4

- Three players on each team, with one goalkeeper each team.
- Same size field as above: 35 x 20
- Goals for goalkeepers are small - cones about 10 feet apart.
- Goals are scored only if ball passes into goal no higher than the goalie's knees.
- Limit game time to five minutes with a 5 minute break for water, then play again.

Challenges for Development:

    a. require 4 passes before shooting on goal.

    b. shots on goal must be with *The Instep* or laces (a power shot).

Helpful Hints

• Goalkeepers can help pass ball around with feet only!

• This restriction on shot height forces players to practice low shots that stay on target.

5 v 5

- Increase team sizes to four field players and one goalkeeper per team.
- Field size now should be 40 x 30 yards.
- Use any of the variations listed above or come up with your own.
- Limit game time to 10 minutes, with 5 minute break, then another 10 minute game.
- End small-sided game time with free play: no limits on passes, touches, etc..

Challenges for Development:

a. limit the number of passes before scoring.
b. each player must touch the ball in passing sequence, including the goalkeeper, before shooting on goal.
c. limit each player's touch of the ball to **two-touch**: one touch to trap ball, one touch to pass.
d. passes must be with the *Inside of Foot* for pass sequences to count.

Helpful Hints

• remaining players can be split up on each team and substituted.

• with more field players, there is less work per player which is why game time is extended.
• this is to allow players to have fun with no restrictions.

6 v 6 and 7 v 7

Note:

Field size for small-sided games of 6 v 6 and 7 v 7 are the same: 50 x 40 yards with two full size goals and two goalkeepers. Use the same limits and games for 6 v 6 and 7 v 7 as outlined for smaller sized games above.

This level of small-sided games is a great way to reproduce live game situations, yet gives each player as much touch of the ball as possible.

Goalkeepers and standard size goals are used. Goalkeepers play in goal as if it were a real game. Another bonus for goalkeepers is a higher number of shots and one-on-one challenges in the goal area, giving them more "realistic" practice in goal.

<u>Coach's Notes</u>

Chapter 3

Practice Checklist

_____ 1. **Soccer Balls**: have enough for 1 ball per player (you may require that each player bring his/her own ball to practice). Be sure players are using the correct size ball for their age group.

   #3 (ages 4-6) #4 (ages 7-10) #5 (ages 11 and up)

_____ 2. **Ball Bag**: to transport balls.

_____ 3. **Ball Pump**: balls need to be inflated to correct poundage (located on a panel on the ball). Carry extra needles.

_____ 4. **Coach's Gear**: Soccer Flats or Athletic Shoes, Shorts, Coach's Shirt, Warm-up top and bottoms for cold weather.

_____ 5. **Whistle**

_____ 6. **Practice Plans**: see Three Month Training Schedule.

_____ 7. **Clipboard**: for practice plans, lists, starting line-ups, substitutions, etc..

_____ 8. **Colored Bibs**: to distinguish one team from another during practice sessions - 10 to 12 bibs of one color should be enough.

_____ 9. **Equipment Bag**: to hold all items above.

_____ 10. **First Aid Kit**:
Athletic tape: 8-10 rolls   Prewrap: 1-2 large rolls
Hydrogen Peroxide   Band-Aid strips:
Analgesic Ointment: extra large 2" x 4"

Cramergesic   various other sizes
Atomic Balm
or
Icey Hot
<u>Medical Scissors</u>   <u>Ace Bandages:</u>
<u>Latex Medical Gloves</u>   3" and 6" wide
<u>First Aid Antibiotic Cream</u>   4" x 4" Gauze Pads

_____ 11. **5 Gallon Water Jug**: it is important to have water at all practices and games in all types of weather. Have players bring their own sports drink and assign a parent to bring oranges on game day.

_____ 12. **Small Container for Crushed Ice**: include several light plastic storage bags to hold ice for sprains and bruises.

_____ 13. 3-Ring Binder to organize and hold the *Survival Manual* for quick, easy reference.

Chapter 4

<u>Three Month Training Schedule</u>

Note:

This schedule is set up for one practice per week, lasting about 1 and 1/2 hours.

Any practice lasting more than 2 hours will begin to **burn-out** players - especially younger ones! At the point when burn-out sets in, no child is going to absorb what you are teaching them anyway, so it is wasted time. Players start to lose their concentration and desire, becoming bored.

Schedule Key:

1.1 = first month . first week
2.1 = second month . first week, etc.

(15 min.) = the time spent on a specified drill or small-sided game.

Coach's Notes

1.1

(15 min.) <u>10 Point Warm up/Stretch</u>

(10 min.) <u>Instep Balance/Ball Control</u>:
    a. each player with ball
    b. roll ball back onto instep (top of foot) and hold there as long as possible
    c. 5 minutes for each foot.

(15 min.) <u>Dribbling/Touch Development</u>:
    a. Instep - push ball about 1 to 2 feet in front of body. Alternate each foot per touch.
    b. split squad in half, first squad dribbles 20 yards, then back. Second squad dribbles 20 yards then back.
    c. repeat.

(15 min.) <u>Inside of Foot Passing</u>:
    a. partners - 5 yards apart - one ball per group of two partners.
    b. pass ball back and forth using **Inside of Foot** technique.
    c. two-touch: trap ball first, then pass.

(20 min.) <u>Small-sided Game</u>:
    a. 4 v 4 (3 field players, 1 'keeper).
    b. field size: two 20 x 35 fields.
    c. goals six yard apart (use cones).
    d. game time: 5 min.; 5 min. rest; repeat.

Helpful Hints

- for correct **instep dribbling**, both feet should be pointing down in a "pigeon toe" technique.
- try to touch ball *each* step.
- start drill by having players *walk*, touching ball each step. When they look comfortable, begin jogging through drill.

- alternate feet each trap/pass.
- *Stay on Toes!*
- trap and pass with *toe up/heel down*.
- *Punch* through middle of ball - foot is off the ground when hitting the ball. Leave foot in air after ball leaves foot.
- keep both knees bent, relaxed.
- arms out for balance.

- field size: two 20 x 35 fields so *all* players play at the same time. 4 goalkeepers - rotate field players as 'keepers for fun!
- use **Inside of Foot** *only* to pass ball around.
- each team should form *triangles* around opponents.

1.2

(15 min.) <u>10 Point Warm up/Stretch</u>

(10 min.) <u>Instep Balance/Ball Control</u>

(15 min.) <u>Dribbling/Touch Development</u>:
   a. **Instep** - gently push ball, touch ball every step (10 min.).
   b. **Inside of Foot** - now dribble 20 yards, pushing ball with the *Inside of Foot*
   (5 min.)

(15 min.) <u>Inside of Foot Passing</u>:
   a. partners - 2 players/1 ball.
   b. ten yards apart.

(20 min.) <u>Small-sided Game:</u>
   a. 4 v 4 as in **1.1** above.
   b. game time: 5 min.; 5 min. rest.
   c. *restriction*: 4 passes before shooting at goal.
   d. *restriction*: shot must be with **Inside of Foot** technique.

<u>Helpful Hints</u>

- repetition reinforces learning skill.
- practice makes **permanent** - constantly check for correctness.
- use same pushing procedure for both *Instep* and *Inside of Foot*.

- passes must be continuous - no interceptions - before being allowed to shoot at goal.
- with *Inside of Foot* shot, ball must travel *below* goalkeeper's knees in order to count.

1.3

(15 min.) <u>10 Point Warm up/Stretch</u>

(15 min.) <u>Instep Balance/Ball Control</u>:
      a. repeat basic drill. (5 min.)
      b. increase Difficulty - hold ball on right instep, then lift into air and catch on left instep and balance. Flip back and forth from one foot to the other.

(15 min.) <u>Dribbling/Touch Development</u>:
      a. repeat **Instep** and **Inside of Foot** drill above.
      b. **Add**: *Back-Pull* with sole of foot.
      c. players *pull* ball 20 yards while moving backwards. (5 min.)

(15 min.) <u>Inside of Foot Passing</u>:
      a. partners, 1 ball, ten yards apart.
      b. **Add**: *Distance Increase/Decrease.*
      c. coach instructs one partner, while passing, to move backwards and forwards - increasing/decreasing distance between partners (10 min.)
      d. This drill should be practiced with *one-touch* of the ball.
      e. accuracy is important and more difficult with *one-touch* passing.
      f. be patient! Accuracy will come with correct repetition.

Helpful Hints

- this drill develops "feel" for the ball.
- ball is not to touch the ground.
- be patient. With encouragement, this skill will develop for every player.

- **stay on toes** as much as possible during this technique.
- alternate feet on each touch.
- this drill is tiring and taxes the calves.

- ball is constantly being passed back and forth while distance between partners changes.
- coach must be visible and vocal when changing distance.
- coach moves, in order to lead, with the line of partners changing distance.
- *Stay on Toes*.
- **Inside of Foot** passing only!
- maintain about 5 yards between each group of partners to keep from crowding.

1.3 Cont'd

(30 min.) <u>Small-sided Game:</u>
    a. 5 v 5 (4 field players/1 'keeper).
    b. field size: 40 x 30.
    c. regular size goals.
    d. passes must be **Inside of Foot**.
    e. 3 consecutive passes before shooting.
    f. **Instep** or **Inside of Foo**t shot.
    g. three 10 minute games.

Helpful Hints

- one field with third team of 5 off and resting.
- if numbers are low for the third team, players from first two teams fill out third team (and will get extra playing time, so be sure to spread it around).

- optional: 5 minutes of "free play" for two teams with the most wins.

1.4

(15 min.) <u>10 Point Warm up/Stretch</u>

(15 min.) <u>Instep Balance/Ball Control</u>:
    a. after 5 minutes of Instep Balance, players begin jug
    gling ball.
    b. juggling should be with the **Instep**.

(15 min.) <u>Instep Passing</u>:
    a. partners, 20 yards apart.
    b. ball hit *easily* with **Instep**.
    c. keep 8 yards distance between groups of partners.

Note: This is a very difficult skill and your players will, most likely, send balls all over the park! *Do not worry.* The eventual benefits of this drill are: **better ball control, low-driven power shots, and improved confidence** with the ball. If you inject this drill now and again, improvement and control will develop.

(20 min.) <u>Add Your Own Drill</u>:
    a. use a favorite drill or game.
    b. work on improving a team weakness.

(25 min.) <u>Small-sided Game</u>:
    a. 7 v 7 (6 field/1 'keeper)
    b. field size: 50 x 40.
    c. standard size goals
    d. game time: 10 min.- 5 min. rest- 10 min.

Helpful Hints

- ball should be juggled with foot **low** to the ground on **Instep** (this is the top of the foot - the laces).

- important to kick ball *easily* in order to control the pass.
- correct **Instep** technique important for keeping pass on the ground and, therefore, under control: ***toes pointed down, ankle locked***.

Small-sided Game
- one field, all players on field.
- if only 1 goalkeeper on team, rotate field players in the other goal (5 minutes each player).
- move and trap ball with **Inside of Foot**.
- players should form *triangles*: player with ball should have at least two partners to pass to at all times.
- players should *spread out*, using whole field to work the ball. It is easier to move/control ball if teammates are spread out (this tactic should **always** be reinforced).

2.1

(15 min.) 10 Point Warm up/Stretch

(15 min.) Instep Balance/Ball Control:
      a. roll ball onto Instep and hold.
      b. alternate lifting ball between left and right foot (5 min.).
      c. Add: juggle ball off of Instep, keeping ball and feet low to the ground (10 min.).

(20 min.) Inside of Foot Passing:
      a. partners are 5-10 yards apart.
      b. passing on ground, changing distance between partners to intensify and lessen the accuracy difficulty.

Add: *Saw Tooth Loop* Passing Drill:
a. two line of players, 5 yards apart, facing each other.
b. each line of players, arms length apart-have them stretch arms to side and touch fingertips.
c. start at one end with one player passing to opposite player, who passes at angle to next opposite down the line, who passes back at an angle to other lines next opposite player . . . all the way to the end. Then reverse the order and come back to beginning doing same thing.
d. **call name** of person to be passed to.

Helpful Hints

- avoid bringing feet above knee height in order to maintain balance and control.

Saw Tooth Loop Drill Illustration

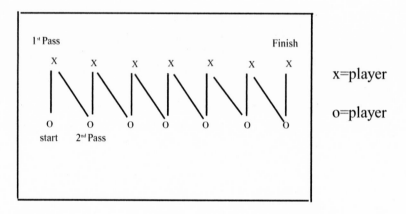

- start with 2-touch. If players are comfortable, go to 1-touch.
- ball is passed with *farthest foot away from ball*. For example: if pass is coming from player's *right* side (at a diagonal line from the set of partners to his/her right), ball is passed using the *left* foot (farthest foot away from the ball) to his/her partner. **Using the *farthest foot* helps insure an accurate pass.**
- all passes are **Inside of Foot**.
- hips are in the direction the pass is going to go.
- developing good talking skills is as important as good passing skills. When on a team, you **must** communicate (sometimes hard to get consistently).

2.1 Cont'd

(15 min.) <u>Add Your Own Drill</u>

(20 min.) <u>Small-sided Game</u>:
        a. 4 v 4 (3 field, 1 'keeper).
        b. field size: 25 x 40 yards.
        c. limit players to 2-touch.
        d. after 5 continuous passes, can take a shot on goal.
        e. game time: 5 min. - winner stays on - next team plays.

Helpful Hints

- focus on *spreading out* in order to form triangles.
- all passing is to be **Inside of Foot**.

2.2

(15 min.) <u>10 Point Warm up/Stretch</u>

(20 min.) <u>Dribbling/Touch Development:</u>
  a. **Instep Push**: toes pointed down, slightly pigeon-toed
     (10 min.).
  b. **Inside of Foot Push** (10 min.).

(10 min.) <u>Saw Tooth Loop Passing Drill</u>

(15 min.) <u>Add Your Own Drill</u>

(20 min.) <u>Inside of Foot Passing Drill</u>

Add: <u>Numbers Passing Drill</u>
  a. split team in half.
  b. field size: 30 x 30 yards.
  c. each team's players have different numbers.
  d. each team tries to keep ball from other team, passing it
     to each other in numbered order starting with #1.
  e. players **must call out** the next number they are to pass
     to so *that* numbered player is ready to receive pass.
     Receiver is forced to pay attention to number count.
  f. if other team steals ball, *they* begin passing sequence.

Helpful Hints

- 20 yards - up and back.
- have players move ball across of body with **inside of right foot** (from right to left), then with **inside of left foot**, move ball across front of body (from left to right) as they dribble to 20 yard mark and back.

- number from #1 to the total number of each team.
- when players get passing in correct sequence correct, have them reverse order from highest number back to #1.
- this is great for developing *talking* among players and *concentration* while playing the game.

2.2 Cont'd

(20 min.) <u>Small-sided Game</u>:
    a. 5 v 5 (4 field, 1 'keeper)
    b. field size: 40 x 30 yards.
    c. standard goal size.
    d. limit players to 2-touch/free passing.
    e. game time: 10 minutes

2.3

(15 min.) <u>10 Point Warm up/Stretch</u>

(15 min.) <u>Instep Balance/Ball Control</u>:
a. give players *free time* for juggling, instep balance, etc..

(15 min.) <u>Inside of Foot Passing</u>:
a. **Saw Tooth Loop** passing drill.

(20 min.) <u>Inside of Foot Passing</u>:
a. **Numbers Passing Drill**

(20 min.) <u>Small-sided Game</u>
a. 4 v 4 (3 field/1 'keeper).
b. **2-touch**: one to trap; one to pass.
c. 5 passes before shooting.
d. game time: 5 min. - rest - repeat.

<u>Helpful Hints</u>

• this time, just focus on 2-touch with players.
• *free passing*. In other words, player can shoot as soon as is able.

• make clear to players this is *free time* for them to work on ball control and getting comfortable having a ball at their feet.

• players must call out next number **loudly**.
• **Inside of Foot** passing technique.

• if enough players, make 3 teams: round-robin play.
• stress **spreading out/triangles**.

2.4

(15 min.) <u>10 Point Warm up/Stretch</u>

(20 min.) <u>Dribbling/Touch Development</u>
Add: Obstacle Course
a. use cones, gear bags, 1 hurdle.
b. measure four 20 yard sides to form a square course.
Description:
a. start and finish are at one corner of course.
b. *first obstacle* is halfway down first side. Lift ball over and follow, jumping over bag. Dribble around first corner, marked by a cone, of the square.
c. *second obstacle* is halfway down second side. Pass ball through two cones, run around outside of them, retrieve ball and move around second corner of square.
d. *third obstacle* is halfway down third side. Same as first obstacle: lift ball and jump over bag.
e. *fourth obstacle* is halfway down fourth side. Push ball through hurdle, jumping over, collecting ball, and dribbling to the finish line - back at the beginning corner.

<u>Helpful Hints</u>

- the hurdle, ideally, should be two plastic tubes (pvc pipe), three feet apart, with thick nylon line strung from top of one tube to the top of the other.

- allow one or two warm up runs to familiarize with course.
- *time* players to see who is fastest.
- *time* players to see who is fastest without making a mistake or missing an obstacle.
- this should be fun and develop dribbling touch.
- make up teams of two to compete against each other.
- ball must stay close to body - should be contacting ball every other touch.
- *Scoop* ball with instep to smoothly lift it over bags. **Do not** kick it over bags.

2.4 Cont'd

(20 min.) <u>Positioning/Field Movement</u>
  Add: Throw-In Game
  a. split team in half.
  b. field size: 40 x 40 yards.
  c. when have possession of ball, team must pass using the proper *throw-in* technique.
  d. must pass 5 times before shooting at goal.
  e. the goal is a cone target that must be hit with a *throw-in* shot.

(25 min.) <u>Small-sided Game</u>
  Add: Mini-Tournament
  a. 4 v 4 (3 field/1 'keeper).
  b. standard size goals.
  c. game time: 5 minute games.
  d. every players spends 2 and 1/2 minutes in goal as their team's 'keeper.

Helpful Hints

- throw-ins must be legal! Poor form turns ball over to opponent.
- can increase number of passes required before shooting.
- this develops stronger throw-in technique.
- this also develops excellent communication and spreading out on the field.
- players usually have fun with this game.

- three teams.
- be sure players realize time will go by quickly.

3.1

(15 min.) <u>10 Point Warm up/Stretch</u>

(15 min.) <u>Instep Balance/Ball Control</u>
    a. roll ball onto **Instep**.
    b. go for highest number of balances per foot (without dropping the ball).

(10 min.) <u>Saw Tooth Loop Passing Drill</u>

(20 min.) <u>Dribbling/Touch Development</u>
    a. *Obstacle Course*

(15 min.) <u>Small-sided Game</u>
    a. 3 v 3 with *no keepers*.
    b. five teams of 3 players each.
    c. 2 fields at 20 x 35 yards each.
    d. game time: 3 min. - new game.

(15 min.) <u>Small-sided Games</u>
    a. 7 v 7 (6 field/1 'keeper).
    b. field size: 40 x 50 yards.
    c. standard goal size.
    d. game time: 15 min. - no break.

Helpful Hints

- goals are scored by hitting 1 cone.
- **Inside of Foot** passing only.
- rotate each team in, remembering the winners.

- four consecutive passes before taking a shot.
- shots can only be taken as **Inside of Foot**. This develops discipline in shooting - composure in front of the goal in order to keep shot on target.

3.2

(15 min.) <u>10 Point Warm up/Stretch</u>

(10 min.) <u>Inside of Foot Passing</u>
      a. partners, one ball between them.
      b. alternate distance between partners while passing.
      c. ball must be passed on ground.

(20 min.) <u>Add Your Own Drill</u>

(15 min.) <u>Numbers Passing Drill</u>

(20 min.) <u>Throw-In Game</u>
(20 min.) <u>Small-sided Game</u>
      a. 4 v 4 (3 field/1 'keeper).

      b. field size: two 20 x 35

      c. fields.goals (cones) six yards apart.

      d. game time: 5 minutes

Helpful Hints

• field players rotate in goalkeeper positions for half of game.

3.3

    (15 min.) <u>10 Point Warm up/Stretch</u>

    (10 min.) <u>Saw Tooth Loop Passing Drill</u>

        a. players pass using *1-touch*.

    (15 min.) <u>Instep Touch/Ball Control</u>

        Add: Instep Volley

        a. partners, 5 yards apart.

        b. one partner on one knee, ready to serve ball to other partner.

        c. ball is *gently* punched back to server's hands.

        d. switch servers at 7-8 minutes.

Helpful Hints

- set-up is same as *Inside of Foot Passing Drill*. Serve ball about **1 foot off the ground** - kicker must keep kicking toes *pointed down*, with foot low to the ground.
  Very important: **ball is not kicked but lightly punched** - otherwise, it will fly off in all directions because the top of the foot (instep) is a hard surface (bone) to control and can easily put too much power behind the ball.

3.3 Cont'd

(30 min.) <u>Small-sided Game Variation</u>

Add: Offense v Defense

a. field size: _ the size of a regulation field. One stan dard goal.

b. <u>Defense</u>: defends goal as if a real game situation.

c. <u>Offense</u>: attacks goal as if a real game situation.

d. coach serves ball to offense, which immediately attacks defense, starting from midfield, at full game speed.

e. after attacking goal, restart again back at half-field.

f. every attack and defense is at *game speed* to make it as realistic as possible.

<u>Helpful Hints</u>

- 1 goalkeeper and four fullbacks in regular field position.
- three forwards: *left wing, right wing, center forward* and two or three midfielders moving down behind forwards as offense attacks.
- this is similar to a half-court game in basketball.
- have Offense take ball down left or right wing and cross or pass it into center to try and score.
- the easiest, less crowded way to move a ball to an opponent's goal is down the outside (flanks). Once down around goal area, look to get ball to player who is open and in position to shoot.
- encourage shooting from all players when around goalie box.

3.4

(15 min.) <u>10 Point Warm up/Stretch</u>

(10 min.) <u>Instep Balance/Ball Control</u>:
  a. allow free time for each player to practice instep jug
     gling and balance.

(15 min.) <u>Dribbling/Touch Development</u>:
  a. **Instep** dribbling - up and back - one time.
  b. **Inside of Foot** dribbling - up and back - one time.
  c. **Back-Pull** with sole of foot - up and back - one time.
  d. **Inside of Foot Static Touch**: players perform for 1
     minute - 1 minute rest - begin again (5 min.).
  e. repeat all four skills above 5 times.

(15 min.) <u>Dribbling/Touch Development</u>:
  a. **Obstacle Course** for time.

(15 min.) <u>Dribbling/Touch Development</u>:
  Add: 1 v 1 competition
  a. partners with one ball.
  b. game is in 10 x 20 yard area.
  c. set up four such areas.
  d. 8 players competing; remaining players resting.
  e. game time: 3 min. - switch groups.

Helpful Hints

• 20 yard distance.

• remember: back pull involves moving backwards, pulling ball with sole of foot, alternating each foot.
• stay on toes. Tap ball between left and right **Inside of Foot** while staying in one place. Ball is directly under player's waist.

• record fastest times around course without a mistake.

• each player takes turn trying to dribble around partner in a restricted area. Area width may be increased.
• a great conditioning drill that develops confidence with ball handling in high pressure situations.
• stress keeping ball *close* to body.
• players need freedom to develop their own ball-handling style. Do not coach at this point.
• this should be a *fun* competition.

3.4 Cont'd

(1 v 1 competition continued):

    f. a point is scored when player with ball dribbles around partner, across end, without going out of the area.

    (20 min.) <u>Finish Practice with Own Game</u>

Helpful Hints

Chapter 5

10 Step Warm Up and Stretch

1. <u>To Get Blood to the Muscles</u>: easy jog around the park or field - one lap.

2. <u>Chest/Shoulder Stretch</u>: lock hands above head, push back. Hold for 20 seconds.

3. <u>Shoulder/Arm Stretch</u>: lock hands behind back, push back. Hold for 20 seconds.

4. <u>Groin Stretch</u>: weight forward on bent left knee, right leg straight and extended back behind body, upper body bends backwards. Hold for 20 seconds. Switch to other leg, repeat.

5. <u>Hamstring/Lower Back Stretch</u>: move to straddle (legs apart) position, grab ankles and gently pull head through legs. Hold for 20 seconds.

6. <u>Calf Stretch</u>: position body as if ready to do a push-up, legs straight, heels on ground. Hold for 20 seconds for each calf.

7. <u>Achilles Stretch</u>: in same position as in #6, bend left knee to raise heel off ground. Hold 20 seconds. Switch to other achilles. Repeat.

8. <u>Inside Thigh Stretch (or Butterfly Stretch)</u>: while sitting, bring soles of both feet together, flaring both knees out. While holding ankles, use elbows to put pressure on inner thighs and push knees down.

9. <u>Lower Back/Buttocks Stretch</u>: cross right leg over a straight left leg, planting right foot next to and outside left knee, left elbow crossed over raised right knee. Push back left against knee. Hold for 20 seconds. Repeat with left leg over straight right leg.

10. <u>Quad Stretch</u>: standing, grab right ankle behind buttocks and push leg back and out. Hold for 20 seconds. Repeat with left leg. Use partner for balance if needed.

Chapter 6

<u>Fundamentals of Goalkeeping</u>

　　　The age group you are coaching dictates what fundamentals you teach young goalkeepers. I've generally used the following guideline when running clinics or camps:

5-8 year olds

• Get used to standing and moving in front of the goal.

• Work on getting the *whole body* behind the ball.

• Catching the ball with hands *behind* it.

• Encourage goalkeepers to have fun and not be concerned about mistakes and poor form (this goes for you too, coach!).

(Catch the ball with both hands *behind* it)

9-11 year olds

- Begin learning basic skills.
- Coach correct *Ready Stance*.
- Correct *Body Positioning In Relation To The Ball And Goal.*
- Correct *Distribution Of The Ball* - kicking/punting technique.

(Positioning in relation to the ball and the goal)

12 and Above

• Reinforcement of above techniques and greater demand for correct execution under pressure.

At the youngest ages, simply look for fearless athletes and try them in goal to see if they take to it. Generally, a coach should experiment with different 'keepers at the early stages. Let them play on the field as well as in goal. From 9-11 years of age, players begin to gravitate to goalkeeping and, at this point, want to spend more time in goal. Also at this stage, more demand and pressure can be placed on the goalkeeper's shoulders and they should respond positively to it.

Many coaches shy away from working with goalkeepers because they are not sure of what to do. The fundamentals in this chapter will give you a solid beginning with your goalkeeper. As with any position and the skills associated with it, the correct foundation must be established first before refinement, experimentation, and advanced goalkeeping techniques can be learned. What you, as a coach, will learn here are the correct:

~ **Goalkeeper "Ready Stance";**
~ **Positioning In Relation To The Ball;**
~ **Distribution Of The Ball;**
~ **Essential Equipment.**

The *Ready Stance*

Points to Remember:

- Legs should be about shoulder width apart.
- Weight is forward on the balls/toes of the feet.
- Hands are out in front of the body about midway between waist and shoulders.
- Palms are out with the fingers spread.
- Knees are slightly bent for balance and agility.

Positioning In Relation To The Ball

Whether a player is just learning the position of goalkeeping or experienced, his/her body positioning in relation to where the ball is on the field is crucial to success in this position. Perhaps the most common error in body positioning is when a goalkeeper loses concentration, begins to "ball watch", and forgets to reposition/adjust as the ball moves to a different area. The result is the goalkeeper being *out-of-position* when a shot is taken, increasing the chance of the opponent scoring a goal.

The instances of your goalkeeper continually being *out-of-position*, in relation to the ball, can be decreased by coaching (and continously reinforcing) the following fundamentals:

- The goalkeeper should always place his/her body between the ball and the goal. This should begin as soon as the ball crosses the midline and enters the 'keeper's half of the field.
- The goalkeeper should constantly check where the goalposts are and where he/she is standing in relation to the posts and where the ball is currently located.
- The goalkeeper needs to continually balance three things:

    1. Where the ball is currently located…
    2. Where the two goalposts are…
    3. Where he/she is standing in relation to the ball's location and the goalposts.

(The goalkeeper places his/her body between the ball and the goal. This
is repeated wherever the ball is located.)

• The goalkeeper should work off an *arc*. Movement in relation to the ball's location is along this arc:

(The "arc" can be closer or further from the goal. The arc in this picture is a good reference to work from.)

Why the arc? Moving in a straight line from goalpost to goalpost, called "staying on your line", leaves the largest scoring pockets or alleys.

Compared to working "off your line" on an arc:

(In this picture, it's hard to see the arc but notice the scoring alley is narrower as the goalkeeper's position is further out and "off the line".)

The *arc* becomes a reference point for the goalkeeper to work from to minimize the opponent's scoring alley.

Working along the arc, which moves the goalkeeper closer to the ball and minimizes the opponent's scoring alley, is commonly referred to as "Cutting Down The Scoring Angle". Using the arc as a base from which to operate, the goalkeeper then decides whether to attack the ball (go out to the opponent with the ball at his/her feet), stand his/her ground, or drop back in case of an attempted chip shot over the goalkeeper's head.

Note: For new goalkeepers, coach them on how to move in front of the goal on the *arc*. Demonstrate the movement for them by moving from one side to the other, then back again. Show your goalkeeper a diagram so they get a *clear* picture of what you are talking about.

1. When the goalkeeper moves on the arc, from one post to the other, the technique for moving is a side shuffle (see pictures). A goal-keeper should always avoid *crossing* his/her feet (this could cause them to trip). As they move across the front of the goal in this side-step fashion, they should be in their *Ready Stance*, ready to react to the shot when it is taken.

(See the sequence of four photos)

2. <u>Coming Off Your Line</u> – this is where a goalkeeper learns to *get off* his goal line and move out to the opponent coming at him with the ball. The closer a 'keeper can get to the ball before the opponent shoots, the narrower the angle (or scoring alley) for the opponent. Also, a confident goalkeeper moving strongly to the ball will, many times, unnerve the opponent. The result can be a mistake made by the opponent with the ball, giving the goalkeeper a chance to get possession of the ball.

<u>Note</u>: Timing is crucial with "coming off your line". If the goalkeeper hesitates, the opponent has more time and space to score, coming out too early or fast can leave the 'keeper vulnerable to a chip shot over his head due to the space opened up *behind* him.

Coach goalkeepers to move out to the ball only when the opponent does not have the ball directly at his or her feet. If the goalkeeper is moving quickly towards the opponent when the ball is at the feet, the opponent can make a move with the ball before the 'keeper has a chance to get set and react.

Basic Key Points To Coach/Remember

1. The goalkeeper moves to the ball only when the opponent is dribbling/moving the ball and causing the ball to be out of reach every couple of steps. It's harder to take a shot when you are dribbling or moving the ball, easier when moving slow and close to the feet.
2. The goalkeeper moves out using short, choppy steps (not long strides) so he/she is ready to react to sudden changes with the ball (shot, pass to someone else, etc.).
3. Body positioning while moving out is the same as the Ready Stance: knees slightly bent, hands open and forward ready to catch, on toes, and leaning forward for quickness with feet shoulder-width apart (for balance).
4. Coach the goalkeeper to use the whole body as a barrier across the path the shot may take:

(Notice how *both* posts are covered by using a proper barrier.)

(Once the ball is within reach, the goalkeeper *smothers* it with the body, wrap-
ping the whole body around the ball for protection against the opponent.)

Important: Goalkeepers **should not** go into the "smothering" of the ball headfirst or feet first. Aside from being a dangerous play that can cause injury, the barrier is narrow and easier to get past.

(Using improper form *narrows* the barrier, opening up scoring alleys. Also, those studs showing on the bottom of the shoe could cause injury and/or draw a penalty against your team.)

5. If you are working with beginning goalkeepers, simply encourage them to "come off the line" at the right time. Refinements can come later. If the goalkeeper lacks the courage to "come off the line" or to smother the ball, first priority is to help them develop their courage. Start slow, having them walk through "coming off the line" and smothering the ball. Increase the realism of this movement (the speed) as your goalkeeper shows confidence. *You* will need to be the opponent with the ball, at first, in order to control the drill intensity level. Later, as your 'keeper becomes stronger, allow teammates to dribble towards the goal and attempt scoring past the goalkeeper

Distribution Of The Ball

Keep distribution of the ball simple for your goalkeeper. A rule of thumb is to have your 'keeper send the ball out towards the left or right sidelines to a teammate (usually an outside midfielder). The goalkeeper should not send the ball up the middle of the field until skilled enough to ensure accuracy. If the kick or throw is short, an opponent might intercept the ball and immediately put pressure on the goalkeeper. Distributing the ball to the outside is the safest move.

In distributing the ball, the goalkeeper can either kick or throw the ball to teammates. Be sure the goalkeeper has a strong arm if you want him/her to throw the ball. Remember to be patient, coach. At first, the execution of either technique may be weak; encourage your 'keeper to improve by reinforcing correct techniques.

As the goalkeeper is developing throwing and kicking techniques, have them use their strongest technique during game time until the other one improves and they can use each interchangeably. Encourage your goalkeeper to find a target (a teammate) and try to get the ball to him/her.

Goalkeeper Equipment

There are no secrets to goalkeeper equipment. However, making sure your goalkeeper has the correct type of equipment can enhance the quality of their play and enjoyment of their experience.

1. **Goalkeeper Jersey**: For today's goalkeepers, many styles of jerseys are available from wild colors and designs to more subdued solid colors. As long as your 'keeper's jersey is not similar to an opponents team colors, whatever type he/she prefers should be acceptable as long as it is an appropriate goalkeeper jersey. The goalkeeper jersey has become a personal *statement* of the 'keeper. Even if you think the style is "horrendous", be positive about their choice.

2. **Goalkeeper Gloves**: Gloves are a very important, if not the most important, piece of equipment for the goalkeeper. They should fit a bit loose but not so loose the gloves will fall off with sudden movement or shaking of the hands. Most gloves are made large and look large to allow more grip-space for catching the ball. There are different surfaces on the palm and fingers for varied climates, so be sure to advise your 'keeper (if he/she does not already know) which *type* of glove to purchase for the climate in your area.

3. **Shoes**: Next to gloves, correct soccer shoes are important for the goalkeeper, especially if you play games in a wet region or where fields are relatively soft. A shoe with studs is extremely important to ensure good traction around the goal area. If you play on hard surfaces, much like the fields in the American southwest, a shoe that has flat traction or smaller studs is important. Shoes with *soft field* studs (longer ones) used on a hard-packed field will result in bruises on the soles of the feet, so advise your players (especially your 'keepers) to choose wisely.

Final Words

Goalkeepers are the most unique players on a soccer team and one of the most important. Goalkeepers are the "last line of defense" and need to be included in all aspects of your team's game plan. Your own goalkeeper can enlighten you, the coach, and the goal scorers at times on how to more effectively beat the opposing team's 'keeper . . . what "moves" and shots are hardest to stop, etc.

Also, it is important for the goalkeeper and his/her fullbacks to work together as a unit. The goalkeeper often sees more of what is happening during an opponent's attack, so passing on information and direction for *tightening* the defensive unit is the 'keeper's responsibility and should be encouraged by the coach. For example, if an opponent is sneaking in behind a fullback, the goalkeeper can call for the fullback to "mark up" the loose player.

The goalkeeper directs his/her defense in order to keep it working together as a unit, so it is very important the defenders and the goalkeeper know each other, work together, and understand they work most effectively as a unit, not as individuals. And, coach, your job is to make this cohesiveness happen and to clarify to the whole defensive unit that working together is the top priority in order to create a good, solid, unbeatable defense.

Chapter 7

<u>Coaching Tips</u>

1. Prior to stepping on the field, make a list of what you want to cover at practice (see **Chapter 4**). Avoid going into practice *blind*. Attach your list (or this manual, which is setup for this purpose) opened to the day's practice and attach it to your clipboard for easy reference during the practice session.
2. Check soccer balls before every practice and game. Make sure they are properly inflated **before** practice and games so time is not wasted. Keep a small hand pump in your bag at all times.
3. When conducting practice, **stand to the side** to direct the drill or session. **Do not** walk through the middle of the playing area unless you stop play to make a point of correction or emphasis. Once made, step back out to side and call for the drill or small-sided game to continue. The reason for this is it is hard to observe what is going on when you are in the middle of it. You get in the way of the players. Also, keep whatever point you need to make **brief!** Covering too many points at one time is confusing to the players. Short, simple steps build to a solid foundation. Remember: *step in, make your point, and step out.*
4. Related and reinforcing #3: avoid walking onto the field during a scrimmage or small-sided game. As stated above, this distracts players and hinders the flow of the game. A sure sign of a rookie coach is to see him/her wandering through the field during the scrimmage or game. If a point
5. needs to be made during a scrimmage (as long as the opposing coach has agreed to this beforehand): *stop play, step onto the field* (go to where you need to make your point), *make it brief and simple, step off or be quickly moving off the field, and restart play.*
6. If a drill or small-sided game you are conducting *breaks down*, do not panic. Stop the drill or session, regroup, and start again. In time, this becomes effortless.
7. If a small-sided game is not *flowing* well (like players bunching

up and crowding around the ball when you want them to spread out) try pulling off a player from each team in order to free up space and "force" the others to spread out. Another technique, in order to keep everyone playing, is to increase the field size to accommodate the number of players being used.

8. Do not be afraid to experiment with your own ideas. Make sure you write them down and make a quick note whether or not they were productive or fun. At every age level, it is important to have *fun* drill and games.

9. Watch top level college and professional games. Note how the players spread out on the field, using the width of the field by moving the ball sideways, not just up and back. Also, note what technique is used most often to pass and trap the ball!

10. Ideally, a soccer team will **move as a unit**: up the field to attack and back down the field to defend.

11. Stress to all players that **everyone** has to play both offense and defense. Forwards do not walk back after they lose possession of the ball to the opponents. They jog back to help their own mid-fielders and defenders regain possession.
Likewise, defenders jog out of the defensive part of the field in order to give support to their team's attack.

12. If your soccer skills are not developed enough to confidently demonstrate a skill, look for a young player on your team who **can demonstrate** the skill and have him/her do it. Usually, there is at least one player on every team who has a good foundation in soccer fundamentals and can demo for you. It makes a young player feel good to be chosen by the coach to demo a skill at practice.

<u>Coach's Notes</u>

Chapter 8

<u>Soccer Related Vocabulary</u>

1. **<u>Inside of Foot</u>**: the inner portion of foot where your arch is located. The most important *bread and butter* skill for a soccer player. Position foot as if it were a golf putter: toes higher than heel, ankle locked, and foot turned out to the side - 90 degrees to the planted foot.
2. **<u>Instep</u>**: the top of your foot. Also, referred to as the laces because shoe laces are located on the instep. *The most powerful shot is taken with the **Instep** or laces.*
3. **<u>Instep Balance</u>**: a technique to develop *touch* with the ball. You hold the ball on the **Instep** (curling the toes up helps hold the ball in place on the Instep) and then gently lift or flip it to the other foot. Just before it touches the other foot, drop the receiving foot a little to absorb or cushion the ball's downward motion. This movement helps prevent the ball from bouncing off the Instep
4. **<u>Instep Technique</u>**: when shooting, passing, or volleying with the Instep (or laces), the toes of the kicking foot must be pointed down and ankle locked (picture how those in gymnastics point their toes). If the toes come up from the point, the ball will rise after the kick and sail upward over, say, the goal. If the
5. ankle is not locked, the kick will lose power, *muffing* the shot.
6. **<u>Small-sided Game</u>**: fewer numbers of players in a restricted area, the playing field, compared to a full-size game of 11 v 11. Small-sided games are one of the most productive training formats for organized soccer.
7. **<u>Spread Out</u>**: a term coaches use to encourage players to use the whole field to work the ball. Bunching of players on the field makes them easier to defend by opponents because they are all in the same area and do not have to be chased in order to be defended or marked.
8. Touch: a player's feel for the ball. How relaxed one is when touching the ball makes all the difference on what the ball does for the player. A player's touch on the ball should be smooth

except for when shooting power shots.

9. **Trap**: a reference to controlling the ball when it is passed to a player. A trap can be performed with the foot, thigh, chest, or even the head. A *relaxed* trapping technique is essential for keeping the ball close to the body and under control.

10. **Vision**: a player's ability to see the game developing while playing and gear his/her decisions based on what is seen and anticipated. Vision usually develops with game playing experience.

Chapter 9

<u>On Field Commands</u>

1. **<u>Away</u>**!   A term used by the goalkeeper to signal to his defenders to clear the ball out of the goal area. A goalkeeper will shout *Away*! when he/she is not able to get to the ball and catch it safely.

2. **<u>Cross</u>**! The action, by a wing or flank player with the ball, of sending a high pass to a teammate in the middle of the field who is in a scoring position. It is quicker to send a cross, in an attempt to shoot on goal, than to perform passing combinations on the ground.

3. **<u>Defense Out</u>**! Another command shouted by the goalkeeper to *remind* his defenders to clear out of the goal area after the ball has moved up field. If the defense walks out, they may keep an opponent onside and give that player an unnecessary advantage should the opponent's team regain control of the ball and counter attack.

4. **<u>Hold</u>**! This command is shouted by an overlapping player who makes a run from behind another teammate who has the ball and instructs that player to *hold*! the ball until he/she runs past. Then, the player with the

5. ball passes to the overlapper. This action floods the opponent's side of the field suddenly with an extra attacking player who can give additional support to the attack.

6. '**<u>Keeper</u>**! Shouted by the goalkeeper when he/she is moving out to catch or fall on the ball. By shouting *'keeper*!, the goalie is informing other teammates that he/she is capable of getting to the ball and *to clear out of the way*. By not listening to this command, a defender or teammate may collide with his/her own goalkeeper, allowing the opponent to get to a dropped ball and score.

7. **Man On!** This command lets a teammate who has possession of the ball know that an opponent is about to *mark up* and attempt to try and steal the ball away. by shouting *Man On!*, a player is acting as the eyes for the other teammate with the ball.

8. **Mark Up**! This phrase is shouted to teammates who need to tightly guard an opponent close to them. By *marking up*, it makes keeping possession of the ball by the opponent difficult.

9. **Overlap!** This movement involves a player running from behind his teammate who has the ball and *overlapping* in order to gain a quick advantage in numbers on the opponent. Usually, the teammate with the ball will pass forward into space, ahead of the overlapping player, so the overlapping player can run onto the ball.

10. **Screen the Ball**! This technique is the same as *shielding the ball*. It amounts to a player with the ball keeping his/her body between an opponent and the ball in order to screen or shield it from being stolen.

11. **Square**! A command shouted to a teammate who has possession of the ball to let him/her know you are off to the side and in an open position to receive the ball should that player in possession become tightly marked and in need of relief.

12. **Switch Sides**! This command, whether shouted from the coach or player, informs the player with the ball to send/pass it to the opposite side of the field. By *switching sides*, a team can immediately move the ball out of a high pressure, tightly marked area, into an open area where it is easier to advance the ball down the field toward the opponent's goal.

Coach's Notes

Chapter 10

<u>Game Day Checklist</u>

____ 1. <u>**Personal Equipment**</u>: game day shirt, shoes, shorts, warm ups, etc..

____ 2. <u>**Equipment Bag**</u>: for personal equipment, pump and needles, clipboard, etc..

____ 3. <u>**Soccer Balls**</u>: your game balls and about four practice/warm up balls. The more balls taken to a game, the greater chance of losing some.

____ 4. <u>**Ball Net/Bag**</u>: to carry balls, keeping them together to avoid losing them.

____ 5. <u>**Ball Pump**</u>: in case one or more balls have lost air since the last practice - it will happen!

____ 6. <u>**Player Rosters**</u>: three copies: one to give to the other team manager, one for the referee, and one for personal use.

____ 7. <u>**Game Plan**</u>: see *Outline* in this manual.

____ 8. <u>**Watch**</u>: to be aware of game time expired and remaining for substitutions and strategy.

____ 9. <u>**5 Gallon Water Jug**</u>: this should be full of iced or cool water. Require your players to bring their own sports drinks.

____ 10. <u>**Paper Cups**</u>: for water.

____ 11. <u>**Official Rules Book**</u>: this should be supplied by your association. Be sure and look through it before your first game.

_____ 12. **First Aid Kit**

_____ 13. **Pen and Pencil:** for notes on your game day plan. For example: keeping track of what time you subbed in certain players, who scored and assisted goals, sudden thoughts on strategy.

_____ 14. **Sliced Oranges**: have parents take turns supplying oranges for the halftime break and after games.

Chapter 11

Game Day Planning Guide

      This game day planning guide is set up with the assumption that everyone on your team will play in the game. Use this guide as a basis from which to experiment with substitutions. Ideally, a player should spend a minimum of 15 minutes on the field at any given time. Less time will make it difficult for the player to warm up and adjust to the flow of the game. Another option is to give each player _ of a game - this can be the first half, second half, or an equal portion of each half. Additionally, avoid substituting waves of players at a time. This will disrupt the flow of the game for your team and become an advantage for the opponent while your players are trying to get in sync with each other.

      The first part of this guide will focus on a basic description of player characteristics for goalkeepers, fullbacks/defenders, halfbacks/midfielders, and forwards/strikers. The second part will be a **Substitution Game Plan**. This game plan is set up as a model to work from and can be photocopied, as with the checklists, in order to make practical use of it.

Player Characteristics per Position

Goalkeeper: this usually takes care of itself. If you do not have a 'keeper, choose a player who has good hand-eye coordination in catching the ball, is flexible and agile (can jump and land well), and no fear of moving into a jumble of bodies in order to catch or fall on the ball. In other words - fearless!

Outside Fullbacks: place your slower defenders on the outside of the defense. They will give up space out there if the opposing wingers are faster. However, this is preferable to giving up space in the middle of the defense in front of the goal. Fullbacks should be strong and have good balance in movement when pressuring/defending.

Middle Fullbacks: these players should be your faster, more experienced defenders. Height can be an advantage in this area when dealing with crosses coming in from the opposing team. Most importantly, the ability to successfully time tackles and have a steady disposition under pressure are ideal characteristics to look for here.

Outside Halfbacks: as with the outside fullbacks, speed is not a necessity when deciding if a player should be positioned outside. Having said that, if you have a number of speedy players, the Outside Halfback position is a good spot, especially if the opponents have fast wing/flank players. However, if you have players that are unsure when reacting to the ball while under pressure and in tight places, placing them in this outside position is usually beneficial because he/she usually adapts well to the increased space and decreased pressure of the outside. If you have players that are able to hold onto the ball while being tightly marked, the middle is the position for them.

Middle/Center Halfback: this is the position to put your most skillful ball handlers. They should be able to keep control of the ball while opponents are tightly marking them. They also should be able to continue the transition of the ball from the defenders to the forwards. Halfbacks are the important link between defense and offense. This is why middle half-backs should be able to dribble, control, and pass the ball while under pressure.

Outside Forward (Wing): players who can dribble or push the ball with speed while maintaining control of it are effective as Outside Forwards. They also should be able to cross the ball with enough power and accuracy to reach the Center Forwards in the middle of the field.

Middle/Center Forward: the most important characteristic of a Center Forward is the desire to score goals. Some forwards feel too much pressure when faced with a goal scoring opportunity and will pass the responsibility off to another player in a less favorable scoring position. A true striker will take a pass and be eager to score. This type of player is said to have a nose for the goal. Another characteristic of a goal scorer is feeling comfortable with his/her back to the goal. In order to receive a pass from the players behind the Center Forward, he/she has to turn around in order to play a vital role in the attack building up from behind. Goal scorers must develop the ability to receive a pass with their backs to the goal, turn, and shoot.

Substitution Game Plan

Starting Line Up:

You may decide to line your team up differently from what is shown below, but this is a starting point/reference to work from. Experiment according to the strengths and weaknesses of your team.

Forwards

left wing   center   right wing

_____   _____   _____

Midfielders

left half   middle   right half

_____   _____   _____

Fullbacks

left back   middle   middle   right back

_____   _____   _____   _____

Goalkeeper

_____

Notes on Substituting

If at your age level and in your league, play is 30 minutes per half, substitute at the halfway mark of the first half, the beginning of the second half, and the halfway mark of the second half.

If you play 40 - 45 minute halves, substitute at the 15 minute mark and again at the 25 - 30 minute mark in each half.

Important aspects to remember about substituting are to keep the numbers small at each sub-interval and to space the intervals out so playing time is fairly equal.

When substituting, try to replace players that are on different parts of the field instead of next to each other. This is because it takes some time for most players to warm up to the speed of the game and if too many new players are next to each other, there will be a large weak spot on the field until these players feel comfortable with the flow of the game.

Coach's Notes

Chapter 12

<u>Coaching the Coach</u>

Focusing on the Player:

As a coach, it is your job to make the practice and game environments safe and enjoyable for the players on your team. Those not directly involved with your team, including parents, should be standing or sitting a reasonable distance from the team bench. This placing of boundaries will minimize the distractions from overzealous parents and spectators and allow you and your players to concentrate on the game. This holds true for all ages except children at the youngest age levels (five to seven years).

Children at this level may need a parent close by for them to feel comfortable and secure while playing. These little players should simply have fun, be allowed to bunch up (beehive), and have coaches and parents cheering for them no matter *what* they do. Structured coaching should not begin until players are eight to nine years of age. Passing to a teammate with something close to the *inside of the foot* technique is sufficient. Small-sided games of 3 v 3, 4 v 4, and 5 v 5 in small areas of 30 x 40 yards will help these youngsters learn to pass and spread out naturally.

During practices and especially games, an effective way to minimize unnecessary encroachment by individuals is to conduct a preseason meeting with parents. At this meeting, outline what you expect from them in the way of parental support during the season. Be specific.

By clearly outlining your wishes and expectations as the team coach early in the soccer season, you have a set of standards to fall back on later should an incident occur with parents or spectators. The parameters are made clear to *all* parents early on. Doing this will diminish many problems that might otherwise appear during the course of your season.

Below is a list of suggestions for establishing reasonable boundaries for you and your players in order to enjoy the game.

- On game day, parents and spectators are to sit no closer than fifteen to twenty yards either side of the player bench or team area.

- Unless there are bleachers set up behind the team bench, do not allow spectators to sit behind the team. Diplomatically ask these people to move to the areas outside of your fifteen – twenty yard boundary.

- The sideline/bench area will stay relatively trouble free during the game if those not directly a part of the team are kept at a distance. If you introduce this concept of a *team area* during game time (and at practice if necessary to do your job), most parents and spectators will be respectful of your wishes. Those that are not can easily be reminded by pointing out where the parent/spectator section is located and directed to that area.

- Complete a sign-up list for oranges and water that parents need to bring each practice and game. If you assign names and hand out the schedule at your first meeting, there will be more *buy-in* by the parents and also you are presenting an efficient and organized persona.

- If a parent has a scheduling conflict with his/her assigned day, they will probably let you know and it can be taken care of at that time. Just make sure *they* are the ones to find someone to switch with them, not you. Learn to delegate this type of administrative detail to the parents in order to leave your time free to focus on coaching.

- New and inexperienced coaches tend to get bogged down with time-consuming duties that can be easily

- passed on to parents. Finding a reliable parent to help is key to keeping your sanity as a coach.

- Do not allow players, unless they are the young five to seven year olds , to stand next to you during game time. Have the players sit together on a bench or on the ground near each other. It is important for team unity that the players stay together. If one or more are standing next to you, they will be distracting you from the game and be perceived by the other players as looking for *special* treatment or attention.

- If players on your team observe another getting this favorable attention, there will be immediate resentment leading to psychological and, eventually, physical breakdown of your team unity. Resentment will develop towards the player receiving special treatment as well as towards you for giving it. Do your best to give all players equal treatment.

- A further distraction that results from allowing players to stand near you is their repeated requests to be substituted into the game. This is extremely annoying and another source of resentment from other players who know better.

- You have a game plan for substitutions and your players need to know this. The way to instruct them is to avoid any player, unless you call them over, from being allowed to stand next to you during the game.

- After a player comes off the field, do not allow him/her to go stand or sit with parents or friends. He/she should go directly to the team bench and sit with the other team members . . . and remain there. Only after the final whistle should you allow the players to sit with or join others.

- Again, the purpose for this is to develop and maintain a sense of unity and teamwork among the team players as well as between you and the team. If your players are spread out and mingling with others not a part of the team, they will be distracted and lack concentration. There is plenty of time for visiting and talking with parents and spectators *after* the game.

• Before halftime arrives, locate a place away from parents and spectators where you can gather the *entire* team for the halftime talk. Some coaches like to keep it loose and allow their players to mingle with others during the halftime break. You will obviously have your preference.

• I have found that by gathering in a relatively quiet spot with few or no distractions, the players stay focused *in the game* and perform more effectively as a team during the second half.

• Also, the players begin to feel what they are doing and participating in is uniquely theirs. A certain amount of pride in the player emerges and, as a coach, you have helped develop that. Outlining this procedure to the players *before* your first game will help things run smoothly as the team comes off the field at halftime.

• Many players are sure they have to readjust clothing or gear as soon as they come off the field. That can wait until the halftime talk is over, just prior to walking back onto the field.

• All players should automatically know there will be a halftime talk and to follow you to the designated spot as soon as the halftime whistle blows.

• If a player has an equipment emergency, have them fix it at the meeting area. Also, make sure players, your assistant, or you have the halftime refreshments

• (players should also have their own bottles with them) for distribution during the talk.

• Never allow a parent or anyone else to coach any of your players, including that parent's own, from the sidelines during a game or practice. One coach, with perhaps an assistant, is enough coach for one team. This also applies to halftime – the team stays together with the coach. It is at times like this you may have to practice *stern diplomacy* and make it clear, without being confrontational, that there is only one coach for your team and that person is you.

• Most of the parents respect this and understand what your job description is – volunteer or paid. Parents that blatantly attempt to coach from the sidelines are a small percentage of the great, supportive parents enjoying watching their children learn and grow from team participation in this or any other sport.

• If you put into practice the concepts and suggestions in this manual, you will know and demonstrate enough knowledge to insure you are teaching your team of youngsters useful fundamentals that they will carry them throughout their playing careers.

• Avoid making any player feel he or she is responsible for the outcome of a game. This philosophy applies equally to wins and losses.

• Pumping up and praising one player over the others can result in several problems:

1. The player, although enjoying the attention, may feel too much pressure and begin to *fail*.

2. The player may develop an attitude that becomes impossible for you to handle as a coach. Also, the other players will think your are "playing favorites" which is another negative distraction.

3. Other players on the team may count on the top player to get the job done and not give their best effort.

4. Team unity will eventually break down, snowballing into uninspired soccer and loss of enjoyment by the players.

Blaming a loss on one player will have some of the same effects listed above as well as resentment towards other team members and you. Generally speaking, the defender or goalie who allowed the ball to get by them and into the net is only the *end result* of another teammate further up field not securing possession of the ball or losing possession of it.

- Although there are amazing individual efforts at times during games, it takes the team to achieve a win or secure a loss. By reminding your young players of this philosophy, you will be helping to lesson the sting of a loss and share the joy of a victory.

- Do not encourage your players to hold grudges against other teams or players. This is irresponsible and unethical as a coach. It is a game not a war. Focus your team's passion or frustration on how to put the ball in the back of the net, not on how to get back at a player or team.

- You will come across other teams whose tactics and attitudes are less than sportsmanlike – count on it. It is how you teach your players to deal with this that will determine your quality as a coach.

- When your players are upset, simply inform them the sweetest revenge is to put the ball in the back of the net and walk home the victor! And, to do it without gloating or flaunting it in front of the other team.

- The proof is always in the performance, not in the posturing.

- Remember: players and parents take your lead, both on the soccer field and on the sidelines. If you demonstrate a lack of composure and respect toward players, opponents, parents, and officials while in your position as a coach, the same will be delivered back to you. As a coach, to gain respect, you must give it – especially when others refuse to show it themselves.

Focusing on the Coach (You):

• <u>When The Game Is Over, *It Is Over!*</u>

Work at leaving the emotions of the game back on the field, not in your head. Some individuals are able to coach a team through the ups and downs of a game and let it go immediately afterwards. Many of us, however, simply struggle with the memories of missed tackles, shots fired wide or over the crossbar, failure of the team to mentally show up on game day, missed chances, unpopular substitutions, botched game plans – the list goes on.

Reflection on the game, good or bad, should be done with emotions calmed and with as much mental separation from the game as possible.

For proven techniques that teach you ways to reduce your emotional extremes under pressure, see *Focus Your Game* at web page:

www.focus-your-game.com

In this way, you can recall the overall flow of the game and determine to what degree the team executed the game plan. From this point, you can make adjustments in your next practice to improve the quality of your team's performance.

As long as you emotionally hold onto the game results, losses and victories, you will struggle with drawing clear, objective conclusions about your team's performance on that day.

• <u>Avoid Getting Bogged Down In Details:</u>

In soccer, it is very easy to intensely watch all the moment-to-moment action of the game and find yourself mentally burdened and frustrated. The game changes quickly with few breaks. Following every movement will cause you to lose sight of the bigger picture and objective.

It is the nature of soccer to have successes and failures occur repeatedly within a short period of time. To expect every attack to result in a goal or every defensive setup to shut down each attack is unrealistic.

Mistakes by your team will happen. Count on it. In this way, when they do occur, instead of downgrading the players involved or stewing over it on the sidelines, you will be calm, aware, and able to see where the breakdown happened and fix it.

One of the most gratifying feelings you will experience as a coach is when you see a weakness during the game, make adjustments, and watch your players explode to the next level as a result of those adjustments. It is difficult to describe the feeling except that you know you have arrived as a coach. Simply magic!

• <u>Work On One Element At A Time:</u>

The layout of the practice schedule in this manual is simple, sequential, yet, repetitive in its approach to teaching fundamentals. The purpose is to give you, the coach, access to what you need to launch a successful season and career as quickly as possible without lengthy explanations and descriptions.

You will have noticed that there is repetition of techniques and drills. The purpose of this folding back over previously practiced elements is to give players frequent opportunities to improve a technique and turn it into a skill.

To introduce a technique, practice it for 15 or 20 minutes, and never revisit it as the season progresses will only allow that technique to fade from lack of use. Folding back and repeating as you move forward will turn that technique into a skill and place it in permanent memory – physically and mentally – so that one day it will be an instinctive reaction for the player.

You will know a technique has become a skill when it is executed repeatedly under the pressure of a game. But, be patient. As a soccer coach, you are working with 11 to 18 individuals all at various levels of development. The trick is to blend all of these players into a relatively cohesive unit. It can do done. But, it will take time.

The most effective and quickest way to develop your team is to cover one element at a time, patiently. Build on each technique as the players show consistent execution. And remember, as you build, fold back now and again on earlier learned techniques in order to reinforce them so the player's skill foundation is solid.

• __Make Time For Yourself:__

At first, the above statement may strike you as trivial. However, time and the managing of it becomes crucial when coaching any sport. Those of you who have coached several seasons can probably relate to weekly routines that leave very little time for relaxation and recuperation. With soccer season, along with many other sports, becoming a year-round time investment, taking care to leave space in your schedule for you (and your significant other!) is high priority.

As a Coach's Coach, I work with clients to outline ways to ensure they maintain a Personal Reserve of time and energy during their soccer season. Doing this ensures you will rise each morning greeting the day instead of "falling into it" or dreading it.

Coaching can drain quite a large amount of energy. After working in the trenches, physically and psychologically, you will gain an appreciation for learning how to balance your schedule in order to enjoy the coaching life *and* your personal life outside of it.

Although there are many areas that can be focused on, below are some immediate suggestions to help clear out needless energy drainers and time wasters.

Tolerations:

Tolerations are those things that we *put up with* on a daily basis that influence the quality of life. They are there and we walk by them or reflect on them constantly without doing anything about them. This is draining. And, when you have a tight schedule that involves coaching a soccer team (or any other team), *tolerations* can contribute heavily to daily burnout.

Example of Tolerations:

- Burned out light bulbs
- Overflowing trashcans
- A car needing a tune-up
- Oil leaks on the driveway
- Bald tires
- Car needing a wash
- A lawn needing mowing
- Broken sprinklers
- Broken hinges on a gate
- Piled up laundry
- Kitchen needing cleaning
- House needing regular cleaning
- Unorganized personal file system
- Soccer/Coaching gear scattered throughout
- the house and garage
- An old computer and peripherals
- Running late to work regularly
- Too many junk food meals
- Skipping meals
- Cluttered closets and bedrooms . . .

This is just a quick list of items that immediately come to mind. When you sit down and really think about all the items you are *tolerating* in daily life, it is an eye-opener. How many times do you say to yourself, "I really need to take care of that . . ." then simply shove whatever *that* is to the growing list of things that need to be taken care of? As we get busier and busier, that wicked list grows longer and our tension grows with it. What results from this mounting tension is not always pretty.

As a soccer coach with a good chunk of time being taken up by your responsibilities, clearing out some of the *tolerations* in your life will greatly enhance your coaching experience.

<u>Suggestions for Eliminating Tolerations:</u>

- Make a list of 10 – 20 items you are currently *tolerating* in your life.

- Study it and decide which items could be quickly and easily fixed or eliminated.

- Try and eliminate one *toleration* a day for a week. If you eliminate ONE *toleration* in a week, this is one more than before you started!

- Notice how you feel after you have eliminated a few easy *tolerations*. Once you have accomplished pruning that list, notice how your free time increases. Also, momentum picks up and the remaining *tolerations* cease to seem so intimidating.

- Notice how you begin to take care of potential *tolerations* as they appear, leaving you with your newly acquired free time.

- What do you do with this free time? Take care of yourself! Spend *quality* time with your significant other or family that is NOT soccer related. Remember, others in your immediate circle of friends and family may not be as excited as you about coaching soccer. If you are coaching your own children, be sure to give them a break from mother/father as the coach – they will love you for it.

- Find some time each day for yourself away from other distractions – including family. This is *your* time! Taking 30 minutes a day to recharge your energy without any outside interruptions is important to maintaining a healthy and positive attitude towards coaching and everything else on your daily agenda.

- Again, go to **www.toquietyourmind.com** and check out *Quiet Your Mind* for a quick 15 minute relaxation exercise that can be done anywhere with excellent results.

• Draw boundaries so people taking up your time that really don't *need* to take it up are kept at a distance. This may sound rude at first, but think of the people infringing on your time right now yet not really adding anything of substance to your life. This is an area of incredible energy drain, yet takes careful consideration of others to avoid insulting them.

• But, of course it seems difficult to make time for you without insulting *someone* along the way. True friends will understand, however, and appreciate the *quality* time you do spend with them because they will know you *want* to spend it with them.

If you find yourself buried under a growing list of responsibilities and commitments, consider trying the steps and suggestions outlined above and trim off that excess. With practice, it will become effortless to streamline your daily routines and, in turn, will increase your energy reserves and improve your attitude throughout your hectic soccer schedule.

AFTERWORD

It is my sincere hope that you have found the ***Soccer Coach! A Survival Manual*** informative and helpful in coaching your team to success. As was stated in the Introduction, this manual is to be used as a *foundation builder* for new coaches and new players, yet is appropriate for experienced coaches to reinforce already developed skills foundations. The skills, techniques, and drills are such that they build good habits in new players and reinforce them in experienced players.

Good luck in your coaching adventure! This game has a way of *getting under your skin.* It is action packed, nonstop play from one end of the field to the other and there is something magical about having a soccer ball at your feet and a field to move it across that is difficult to express in words. All one need do, as *you* well know, is to step onto a field, saturated with the smell of newly cut grass, and drop a soccer ball at your feet . . .

Please feel free to email with suggestions, comments, or stories to share at the address below.

In the Spirit of the Game . . .

Chris Charles Hampton

Background:

Chris Hampton is a seasoned coach with over twenty years experience building, from the ground up, both boys and girls high school soccer teams, managing his own summer soccer camps from ages 5 to 19, training club teams and individuals, and teaching classes covering various aspects of coaching the game.

Coach Hampton's playing days took him from Ohio, Alabama, Arizona, England, Alaska, Rollins College in Florida, to southern California. He has coached in such diverse climates as Alaska, Florida, Alabama, Arizona, England, and California, taught and coached in the public school system, and finds that this varied experience has enabled him to effectively work with coaches from all over the global soccer community.

In the early 1980's, Coach Hampton was one of only a handful of American coaches awarded the English Football Association Preliminary Coaching License under the direction of Alan Wade. He also attended the English F. A. Full License Course at The National Sports Centre, Lilleshulle Hall, England under the direction of Charles Hughes.

*Be sure to bookmark and return to...

www.yoursoccercoach.com

...now and again to discover what's new for both experienced and beginning soccer coaches.

To Contact Coach Hampton:

      Phone: 760-961-1313
      Website: www.yoursoccercoach.com
      E-mail: yoursoccercoach@yahoo.com

Printed in the United States
21185LVS00007B/275